WARRIORS LEGENDS ALPHABET

Words by Robin Feiner

A is for **Al** Attles.
The face of the franchise,
Attles first joined the
Warriors in 1960 and
holdsthe record for longest-
ever unbroken association
with an NBA team. This
legend has been The
Destroyer as a player,
a title-winning coach, and
a beloved ambassador to
the community.

B is for Rick **B**arry.
This scoring machine was a fierce competitor with a fiery attitude. Behind strong shooting and legendary underhanded free throws, Barry was an All-Star in his eight 1960s and '70s Warriors seasons. He also led an underdog Golden State team to the 1975 title.

C is for Stephen **C**urry. Chef Steph cooked up a Warriors dynasty. This legend changed the NBA by draining threes from just about every-where. The ultimate teammate, Curry led the Warriors to six Finals, four titles, and a record 73-win season from 2014–22. Those who doubted his size look silly now.

D is for Baron **D**avis. This sturdy point guard had a huge impact on Golden State from 2004–08. Behind his leadership and energy, the We Believe Warriors broke a 12-year playoff drought in 2007. Davis ran a high-powered offense that stunned the top-seeded Dallas Mavericks in a legendary first round upset.

E is for Monta **E**llis.
His fun, loose play didn't always lead to wins. But he brought life to Golden State during a mostly losing era. Ellis grew into a high-scoring shooting guard over six-plus Warriors seasons. His legendary status was symbolized by fans' anger over his 2012 trade.

F is for Eric 'Sleepy' Floyd. Floyd earned his only All-Star selection during the 1986–87 season. But he saved his best for the playoffs. Facing elimination in Game 4 of the second round, Floyd erupted for 29 points in a legendary fourth quarter against the heavily favored Showtime Lakers.

Gg

G is for Draymond **G**reen. The defensive backbone of the Warriors dynasty of the 2000s and 2010s, DG is never afraid to say what's on his mind. While Steph and Klay get a lot of the spotlight, Green's flexibility on both ends of the court unlocked legendary small-ball success.

H is for Tim **H**ardaway.
This exciting scorer and his
legendary crossover helped
spark the beloved Run
TMC trio of the early 1990s.
Hardaway's relentless style
of play and excellent passing
skills earned him three
All-Star selections in five
full Warriors seasons.

I is for Andre Iguodala. The main man for years in Philly, Iggy's role changed greatly when he came to Golden State in 2013. His stats dropped. But his winning impact was huge. The ultimate glue guy, this legend's 2015 Finals MVP performance showed how crucial he was to the Warriors.

J is for **J**amaal Wilkes. This legend's shot looked weird. And many considered him too thin for the NBA. But the 1974–75 Rookie of the Year and title winner fit seamlessly into coach Al Attles' team-first philosophy. Wilkes was also an All-Star and a two-time All-Defense Team member before leaving for the Lakers in 1977.

K is for Kevin Durant. The Slim Reaper joined Golden State in 2016, striking fear into fans of the other 29 teams. A legendary scorer, two-time Finals MVP, and NBA champion, KD is one of the most adaptable superstars in NBA history.

L is for Joe Lacob.
One of the men who put the Warriors light-years ahead of the rest of the league, Lacob's legendary willingness to spend helped keep the team's brightest stars together. His ownership journey took him from boos at Chris Mullin's jersey retirement ceremony to championship cheers from millions of fans.

M is for Chris **M**ullin.
A legendary lefty, Mullin
was an absolute warrior
for the Warriors. After over-
coming personal issues off
the court, this Hall-of-Famer's
smooth jumper and tireless
work ethic made him a fan
favorite. He, Mitch Richmond,
and Tim Hardaway's RUN TMC
era is one of the franchise's
most memorable.

**N is for Don Nelson.
The legendary architect of
Nellie Ball, this coach helped
change how the game is
played. Nelson's sensational,
speedy, small-ball style really
took off when he coached
the early '90s Warriors. All
gas, no brakes – and a ton
of fun for fans.**

O is for Billy **O**wens. Don Nelson thought this forward would add size and skill to his run-and-gun Nellie Ball team. But trading beloved Mitch Richmond for Owens proved to be a legendary misfire. Owens made the 1991–92 All-Rookie Team. But Golden State missed the playoffs in all three of his seasons with the Warriors.

P is for Paul Arizin. Pitchin' Paul's legendary jumper helped transform basketball in the 1950s and '60s. Arizin was a skilled scorer when points were at a premium. A one-team player and All-Star in each of his 10 seasons, this forward led the Philadelphia Warriors to the 1956 championship.

Q is for Klay's **Q**uarter. Klay Thompson's legendary lightning-quick release helped him form an explosive backcourt duo with Splash Brother Steph Curry. Klay's sweet shooting was on full display during a historic third quarter on January 23, 2015, when he caught fire and dropped an NBA-record 37 points.

R is for Mitch **R**ichmond. Warriors fans were robbed of more time with this legend when he was traded after just three seasons with Golden State. The 1988–89 Rookie of the Year, Richmond's competitive spirit, physicality, and ability to score in various ways were crucial to the high-flying Run TMC era.

S is for **S**teve Kerr. Arriving as a first-time head coach in 2015, Kerr turned a great foundation into a dynasty. This legend embraced his players' strengths and personalities – enduring plenty of turnovers and technicals along the way – to guide the Warriors to four titles in six Finals appearances.

T is for Nate **T**hurmond. A legendary two-way star, towering Nate the Great earned seven All-Star and five All-Defense Team nods across 11 Warriors seasons from 1963–74. This amazing rebounder and shot blocker was a giant off the court, too, making a difference in San Francisco communities after retiring.

U is for Ekpe Udoh.
With one of their few recent lottery picks, the Warriors chose Udoh sixth overall in 2010. He didn't produce on the court. But he was part of the 2012 trade package that brought rugged Australian center Andrew Bogut to the Warriors.

V is for **V**onteego Cummings. Only loyal fans who suffered through some dark losing days will remember Cummings. Golden State won just 36 games in this guard's two seasons with the team from 1999–2001. But it's that journey that makes the championships that followed all the more legendary.

W is for **W**ilt Chamberlain. An all-time great, Wilt the Stilt dominated with superior athleticism and skill during his 1959–65 Warriors career. He averaged an incredible 50 points and 25 rebounds per game during the 1961–62 season, including his legendary 100-point performance. The NBA was forced to change its rules due to The Big Dipper's unstoppable play.

X is for Ale**x** Hannum. The 1963–64 Coach of the Year, Hannum led a team featuring Warriors legends Wilt Chamberlain, Nate Thurmond, and Al Attles to the NBA Finals. But the good times wouldn't last. Hannum and Chamberlain went from icons to enemies when they joined the Philadelphia 76ers who defeated the Warriors for the 1967 title.

**Y is for Brett Yamaguchi.
Yamaguchi is directly
responsible for helping
millions of Warriors fans
create legendary memories –
despite never playing a single
minute for the team. For more
than 25 years, Yamaguchi
orchestrated the gameday
experience for fans who
provided a real home-court
advantage at Oracle Arena.**

Z is for **Z**aza Pachulia. Dirty or dedicated depending on who you ask, Pachulia left a mark on opponents and an impression on Warriors fans during his two title-winning seasons from 2016–18. His legendary picks helped free up Steph, Klay, and KD to fire away.

The ever-expanding legendary library

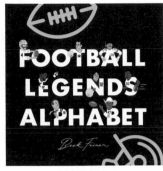

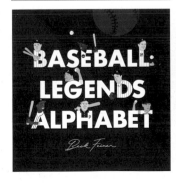

EXPLORE THESE LEGENDARY ALPHABETS & MORE AT WWW.ALPHABETLEGENDS.COM

WARRIORS LEGENDS ALPHABET
www.alphabetlegends.com

Published by Alphabet Legends Pty Ltd in 2023
Created by Beck Feiner
Copyright © Alphabet Legends Pty Ltd 2023

Printed and bound in China.

9780645851502

ALPHABET LEGENDS